INTRODUCTION

THE DEVIL WALKED BESIDE ME
WHEN I WAS JUST A CHILD
HE BRIBED ME AND HE COAXED ME
TO LURE ME TO HIS SIDE
HE GAVE ME SWEETS AND LOTS OF TREATS
HE SAID I SHOULD'NT TELL
ABOUT THE THINGS HE DONE TO ME
OR I WOULD GO TO HELL
THE EVIL THAT'S STILL LURKING
AT THE FARSIDE OF MY MIND
ARE THE SCARS OF CHILDHOOD MEMORIES
LONG SINCE LEFT BEHIND.

As I stood over the frail old man that I was nursing on his sickbed I looked at him and felt a sense of pity. He stared back at me with his sad wrinkled face and his hollow eyes and he had no recollection of who I was but I knew him. As I mopped his fevered brow and fed him sips of water a sickness welled up in the very pit of my stomach as the memories kept flooding back.

I would have just turned twelve that autumn as bonfire night approached and it changed the course of my life forever. I had no reason to fear him as he was my father's friend. I thought nothing of the times he had held me on his knee cradling and rocking me gently back and forth and as I grew he would put his arm around me squeezing and hugging me and I never realised then what he was doing as he cupped my already budding breasts when his arms went around me.

I recall the blazing fire and my friend and I holding the sparklers, making patterns as we twirled them in the air. I remember even the smell of the potatoes baking at the base of the fire wrapped cosily in their foil protection. Sometime later my Mother and the others went into the house leaving my friend and me to watch the dying embers safe or so they thought in the knowledge that he would be outside with us to take care.

Sitting on something either side of him I recall him cradling us both in his arms, as we shivered in the cold night air watching the fire slowly burn out. I think that our hands must have been cold or something as he shoved them between his legs to keep them warm and we felt a movement, we looked bewildered at each other when he told us it was nothing to be frightened of.

Then as he showed us what it was that had moved he wrapped our small hands around it cupped in his own big hands as he moved them up and down to relieve himself, catching the spill in a handkerchief that he hastily pulled from his pocket. Kissing us both as he finished and saying how special we were Thrusting a pound note into our hands whilst he told us that we should say nothing or we would be in big trouble from our mums.

As time went on a pattern emerged and afterward we would very quickly spend our money, stuffing our faces with the sweets and chocolates lest we be found out. As time went on the touching increased and the pain would be followed always with the sickness welling up inside me in the very pit of my stomach finding comfort only from the lovely sweets and chocolate that would later follow. After time my friend stopped being there but I never managed to escape as he was always hanging around, like part of the family.

I wanted to say something, I wanted to be found out, and I wanted it to stop. I tried being bad stealing money from my mother's purse or my father's pockets to justify the sweets. Why wouldn't they scold me make me stay in my room? They would just say I was naughty and tell people I was going through a phase and I always seemed to get away with it and sent on my way. I tried to be really bad and I wanted to be punished I wanted it to stop but it wouldn't go away.

Springing back again to reality and the situation now in hand, I looked at the man and wanted to punish him for what he had once done. I wanted him to know who I was and to feel the pain that he had inflicted on this once small girl.

Sitting him upright to adjust his pillows I stood motionless as I held the pillow in my hand and desperately wanted to press it down on to his tired face so that he too would struggle and feel the pain.

Shook from my daze I screamed as he reached out and grasped at my arm. The scream brought my colleagues running and as the nurse in charged asked me what had happened I broke down in a frenzy of tears as the pain and the sadness all came out. As my own dear father was at the time on his deathbed it was easy for my colleagues to assume it had all been too much for me and they ushered me off to a quiet room leaving me to calm down.

Try as I might I could not calm and yes the sadness I felt for my father was part of the pain but I could hold the real pain in no more. As I told my boss parts of it in-between uncontrollable bouts of crying and with a stammering voice, she put her arm around me and told me that it wasn't too late to get something done.

Days later I got a visit from a liaison officer on the Police child protection league and as she talked me through the events of my past, she assured me that it was not to late to bring this man to justice. Statements were made not only from me but from other women that he had also violated during their childhood years. Including somewhat reluctantly a statement from the friend who had shared that bonfire nights experience with me.

It was so good once again to be in contact with her after all these years and as we talked of our lives in-between, it was easy to see that the path we both followed was part of the suffering that he had inflicted as our lives both followed a course of physical and mental abuse from the types of men we had chosen to love. I was happy that I had managed to convince her to press charges and happy to have her friendship and support.

During the visits from the liaison officer it seems that she also talked to my Mother to try and get a picture of where and how this man came into our lives and why I would be left with him. After she had talked to her I dreaded visiting her as it took me back to the once guilty child I had been. Although the officer assured me I was not the guilty party it didn't make it any easier having to face my Mum with the recollections of the past.

I had hoped somehow she might understand and tell me that it was alright. I wanted her to hold me and comfort me like she should have done then. I wanted her to make it all better. I wanted her to tell me it was alright. Instead I was greeted like a scolded child and asked what I had been thinking of to let this man touch me. The confrontation turned into a shouting match between my Mother and me with us both blaming each other. I couldn't believe that she wouldn't have known what type of man he was and left me in his care.

I turned the blame to her it was her fault for letting it happen. Things were bitter and cold between us and only then got back on track following my father's sudden death when I had to be there to comfort her and to be her strength in her hour of need. Although things between us had improved the incidents of the past and the police officers visit was never mentioned again. One of the strange things being that if she mentioned a pedophile that had been in the paper or on the news she couldn't even see the connection or realise that I had lived the experience.

I needed closure and I wasn't going to get it from her. Neither did it seem that I would be getting it elsewhere as just before the court hearing the man in question was taken ill and everything had to be put on hold. The man was terminally ill with cancer and being in such a position it seemed the courts would not favorably put him under the stressful ordeal of a hearing as it was not in their best interests.

I felt so angry and hurt to think that having buried the pains of my childhood only to dig them all up again they would be left to fester away in my mind causing me continuous pain. No amount of anyone telling me he was suffering now made it any easier he was on his way to death and escape. If there was such a place I hoped that he suffered eternally in the fires of hell.

When I read of his death and people said poor old so and so is dead it made me feel angry. For some reason they thought he was the pillar of the community, what a nice bloke he was helped all the old dears with their shopping, do anyone a favor and didn't he love the kiddies. Didn't he just! This was one kiddie's life he truly ruined.

RUNAWAY

Escape from the memories was hard but escape from him back then even more so. Not even sure how I actually did get away but recall another older man that took kindly to me and although I was falling into a similar trap I didn't see it back then. I would have been around fourteen years old and the man in his mid twenties, I was a typical teenager and he was a fairground worker.

I first set eyes on him when he was giving out leaflets and as he thrust one into my hand he said come along tonight free rides for pretty girls like you. That was it I was smitten. Coaxing my cousin into going with me we searched the fairground for a glimpse of him and then found him working on the waltzers. I watched as he clung to the back of the car spinning the screaming girls around until they could take no more.

He was magnificent in tight jeans and leather jacket with his long dark wavy hair and his unshaven face. I gazed constantly at him as the rides spun and the music played and felt sad as he seemed never once to look my way. My cousin had to leave as there was a bus to catch and as we walked away from the rail he swiftly jumped from the moving platform and put his hand on the rail trapping us as he did so. "Going so soon" he said. "Jump on "

I tried to persuade my cousin to stay a while longer but after just one ride she left for her bus. I know now that I should have left with her but caught up in the moment and reveling in the attention I stayed.

At the end of each ride he would come over to me and gently stroke my hair telling me how beautiful I was and just how much he wanted me. I really thought this must be love. When the rides shut down he took me back to his trailer and took me pleasurably to places I had never been.

I went home that night and lied blatantly to my mother about missing the bus and as long as I was home now she seemed ok with it. About this time I had managed to make friends with a rather gullible girl who I easily persuaded to convince my mother I was out with her. Happy to have my friendship and a little time with me the girl was easily convinced. As long as I was home at the allocated time my mum would be none the wiser.

Over the next two weeks I saw the fairground man every night and felt content to be held by him and to be told just how much he loved me. He said that I was special and had a gift. He said he could look after me and dress me in fine clothes. He said I was his little Queen. I loved his body and I was fascinated by the pictures all over his skin and the gold ring in his ear. He made me feel special and if he told me black was white I would have believed him.

Soon the time for the fairground to leave came but only to the next town so the meetings continued for yet another two weeks. When he had to pack up after that town and move on my life felt like it was going to end and when he said I could go with him and that he would always be there to take care of me I knew I had to leave with him. He said that I had a quality about me and he knew of a way that I could make us both a great deal of money.

He said that I had to go then and there but I couldn't leave just like that I had to go home and get my things so he said he would wait but he didn't and when I returned to the field where the fairground had once stood I felt empty and lost , sobbing I made my way back home.

For days I sat in my room not wanting to go out apart from school. Sticking to my lessons and distancing myself from everyone, I starved myself and making myself ill in the process. My mother just put it down to puberty and left me to it; Dad just worked and didn't even seem to notice. Then one day the gullible friend came round and though I could not be bothered with her I saw her all the same. Pleased afterwards that I had as she had a letter for me from him, the fairground man I remember I had given him her address one time should he need to contact me.

The letter was post marked Sheffield and he said that he had to see me. Suddenly my spirits lifted and as long as I was happy and getting out with my friend again I assume my mother must have thought I had got over my little spell. Managing to convince my mother I was staying with my friend for the weekend there were no questions asked. Shoving a few clothes and toiletries in a bag I took my savings out of my bank and bought a one way ticket to Sheffield.

Catching the train all I could think about was that I was soon going to see him and start my new life. Wrapped up in it all I gave no thought to what my parents would think or feel when I didn't go home. The staff and passengers on the train never questioned me so how could I be doing anything wrong. Arriving in Sheffield I was directed through an underground tunnel that brought me into the heart of the city.

This place was like nothing I had ever seen before so vast and so busy with the crowds bustling and the noisy flow of the traffic. I remember asking a man selling newspapers where a certain park was and followed the directions I was given.

Looking round for the waltzers I eventually found who I was looking for. As I called his name he turned and ran to me sweeping me up in his arms calling me his little Queen and telling me how pleased he was to have me back with him. He kept me with him all day showing me off to his friends and telling them how special I was. As the day turned to night he told me that he had to start closing up and cleaning round and that he would be with me later. Ushering me to a large caravan he told me I could get showered and gave me a silk nightdress that he wanted me to put on.

Once in the caravan I found it to be filled with other girls some perhaps my age some a little older. One of them was really nice to me and gave me a large glass of fizzy drink that she said was wine. I had never drank wine before and found it a little sharp with a horrible flowery smell. I couldn't drink it and the girl got nasty with me telling me that I had to before the men came. I wondered what men she meant and thought only of my special man coming.

When he did come he asked why I hadn't drank the Gin fizz and when I said I didn't like the taste he said he would find some vodka. He told me to put the nightdress on but I didn't want to. This didn't feel like all our other times together why had he changed and why was he being so forceful. He returned with the drink and with him an overgrown man of about fifty.

He said I should make him happy like I used to him then I could be with him all night and he would love me once again like I wanted him to. The fat man sat beside me and slobbered all over I and I felt sick like I used to with the bonfire man. I knew what he wanted and I couldn't do it. Making an excuse to go to the toilet and once in there I climbed out of the window and ran like id never ran before.

I found myself in a back street and realised that I had left my bag and my money in the caravan. I didn't know where I was and I didn't know what to do. I walked for what seemed like ages and was approached by a scruffy old woman carrying a load of bags and blankets. Somehow she managed to persuade me to sit with her and as I snuggled up to her I must have fell asleep as when I opened my eyes it was daylight. I remember thinking how kind she was and as she got me a cup of tea and a bacon sandwich from a roadside van she told me that unless I wanted to end up like her that I ought to go home.

Heading for the train I never even thought of how I was going to pay for a ticket and when I explained to the guard that I didn't have any money he brought a policeman who asked me where I lived and gave me a ticket home. For the entire journey I cried and all I could think of was that I wanted to get back home. Finally outside my door I stood half afraid to go in wanting to tell my parents of my dreadful ordeal yet concocting some story in my head about the great weekend I had had with my friend.

I had hardly set foot in the living room and about to tell my Mum of the weekend when the back of her hand came bouncing off the side of my face. As she screamed at me telling me what a little whore I was she waved the Sheffield letter in my face and said she knew what I had done

She said the police had been to see her and as she hit me again full in the front of my face the blood flowed from my nose and my father shouted at her to leave me alone. When he finally pulled her off me I ran to my room where I stayed till I cried myself to sleep. Refusing for days after to come out except for meals, then making myself sick afterward wanting to die and never grow up. After that I never had any friends and I never went out anywhere unless my Mother or both parents were with me. I was dragged to bingo, shops and even to the pub. So it became a way of life.

NO WISER

I was a quiet girl and for the first time in ages my mother was showing me real attention and affection. It was on one of these nights out with my Mother and her friends that I met my first real boyfriend. The night in particular was her works night out and she introduced him to me telling me what a nice lad he was. It would seem that he worked on the factory on the line next to her and when he displayed an interest in me she pushed it and encouraged him to phone and take me out.

He seemed nice and Mum knew him so it had to be ok. At seventeen he was just two years older than me and Mum said that he should respect me. It seemed he did as other than kissing me and holding my hand he made no attempts to touch me in any other way or in intimate areas of my body. I couldn't really understand this as it didn't seem normal and I would come on to him in ways that I had been shown but he wouldn't respond.

Otherwise he seemed to dote on me and on his pay day could barely wait to take me shopping and buy me new outfits in which he would proudly parade me around the town and in front of his friends. On these occasions he made me feel good about myself and he made me feel wanted. In time my self-esteem became high and my confidence soured. I knew I looked good and I knew that other boys noticed me I enjoyed the feeling that this would bring and regularly made eye contact and smiled at these boys. When we were out he seemed fine about this and reveled in the idea that he had his trophy by his side.

However after time and once behind closed doors our relationship started to take on a very different turn. Alone in his room he would pin me down sitting on top of me his legs astride whilst holding my arms above my head and whilst I struggled for freedom he would call me a little slut. He said I wanted these boys and accused me of cheating on him with them. But no matter how much I struggled or swore to him that I wanted only him and that I had not been unfaithful. He would not let go until he had finally reduced me to tears then he would hold me tight and tell me how much he loved me and how we would always be together. The worse it got the more that I would learn to cope by living only for those after cuddles and those gentle persuasive words of love.

In public and in front of our families I kept up the charade and everyone said that we made a good match. Indeed on the surface we did and to the unassuming eye we would seem like the perfect boy girl next door couple. As time went on I got so that I dare not even look sideways at another male in an endeavor to stop the torture but should one look at me I would still go through it having been accused of encouraging the glance. Before long the pinning down sessions became sexual with him becoming aroused the more that I struggle. The cuddles, the outcome would be my way of gratification.

He would even encourage me to entice these males and they eventually became a part of the ritual at first just watching whilst they satisfied themselves and eventually in turn having their own go on top of me whilst I shut my eyes and bit back the tears knowing that I would eventually end up in his arms for the night and that he would love me again.

As he ushered his friends off apologising for my lack of group participation I gathered my senses and ran off. Eventually reaching my aunts house and spilling the whole story out to her. My aunt was so angry but surprisingly not with me and as she dragged me round to his house and confronted him he withered like a small plant dying in the heat and I felt free at last.

Soon after this I left school and got my first job on a sweet counter at a large department store. I felt nervous and found it difficult to mix coping only with the stress by the secret binging of the sweets when I went under the counter to replenish the stock. The place was buzzing with the sound of happy boys and girls and though I longed to be part of the group I kept myself to myself and busied myself by reading in my breaks and speaking only to senior staff members and the lads from the stockroom when they spoke to me.

After awhile I became friendly with a girl, maybe a year or as older than me and felt content in her company as she brought me out of my shell. I admired the way in which she dressed and her soft wavy hair and before long I was modeling myself on her and following her guise. She introduced me to her friends and to a life of parties and binge drinking but nothing sexual.

She had me right where she wanted me and I adored her. I adored even more her boyfriend and wanted the affection that he gave her to be mine. He never touched me in any wrong or disgusting way even though I longed for him to do so. I wanted him so badly, that I would practically throw myself at him wanting his response and becoming hurt and angry when he laughed and called me little sister.

I wanted to be part of the love shared and getting no response I distanced myself from them and started to mix with others in the group. Others including his brother who did take advantage of my charms and when I saw how angry this made the elder I would do it all the more trying to hurt him and not realising that I was actually only hurting myself. Some of the group smoked dope and would offer me some but I could never quite grasp it so instead loosened up on the vodka until one day when another group of girls introduced me to the effects of sniffing shoe glue.

So I left the safety of my friend and her boyfriend whilst I started to explore another type of life. Getting into the lifestyle I enjoyed the company and the attention that I received and by night would participate in group sex and lesbian activities, whilst by day I continued working on that sweet counter. Once again finding comfort from the sweet taste of the chocolate on my palette as it slid down my throat and in a way comforted me and washed away the shame. I felt trapped in a situation that I would not let myself get out of. I missed my two friends and felt the pain of the life that I had since thrown away. I had it all friends' attention a kind of love yet I started to hate it and went along with it only through the manipulation of the stronger members of the group. This promiscuous lifestyle must have gone on until the group drifted and its members went on their separate ways.

A BOY TO LOVE

I was again in limbo not knowing which of the roads to take. I wanted people, money, nice things but mostly I wanted love someone or something all my own. It was the summer of my sixteenth year that fate or cunning took a turn and my life went off in a different direction and I found somebody to love. Not a man but a child my own child my son.

The father of the child was not at first pre selected. In fact our relationship started off quite by accident when I turned up in place of a friend who should have been on a blind date. Romantic it was not! I showed up at a disco to tell him she was ill and he promptly shoved her ticket in my hand and said "you better have this then" From what I recall I had a reasonable time dancing and mingling with a few people once the drink had got into my system and taken off the edge. I really don't remember seeing much of him apart from having the odd drink shoved in my hand when he wasn't propping up the bar or chatting up the girls. I remember the lift home as he had a van with a few blankets shoved in the back and no prizes for guessing where we ended up.

He took me home and for the next few weeks we started seeing each other on a regular basis and that was it I was besotted. He was like a regular bloke. He played football and I watched in awe as he tackled and kicked his way through the game. I made friends with his team mates and their partners, we went to dances and movies together and it seemed to me to be for once a normal life. I loved him and assume he loved me. We went places together, we talked, we were friends and we stayed over at each others houses alternative weekends becoming part of each others families. It was a good life.

I remember exactly when I conceived it was a month after my seventeenth birthday and it was on my bedroom floor. For two whole months I had stopped taking my pill and had made my mind up to have a child to make sure that we would always be together. Me who had done so many things in my short lifetime was really very naive not thinking of the effect that any of it might have on people's lives or indeed the life of the child. When my period didn't show I was so happy yet at the same time a little afraid and not daring to tell a soul. When the second period failed to show and the sickness started I knew that I had conceived. For a while I kept it to myself not knowing how to tell anyone and assuming it would reach its time and just be born and people would just have to deal with it.

Eventually the first person that I told was him, he was the daddy and he had a right to know. I remember it well we were at a football match and I had got chatting to a traveller girl who was camped nearby. At halftime I never really noticed the way he looked at her and the way he just ignored me when I said I had something to tell him. Then at the end of the game when he stood chatting to her on the sideline I took his word for it when he said he was arranging a date for his friend and that we were all meeting up later for a foursome.

When we got home I tried again to tell him and he said that it could wait, he dropped me home and said that he would collect me later so that the four of us could go out and we would talk then. I really wanted it to be just us and I planned in my head a picture of how I would tell him and how he would be delighted and we could start making our future plans. As the evening progressed I sat home waiting for him to show and as the clock ticked away from 7pm to 9.30 pm I started to feel sick with the worry that something dreadful must have happened.

When his mother answered the phone and said he had left ages ago to go to his mates, I phoned his mates house only to be told that he had actually gone abroad with his fathers family. All sorts of pictures conjured up in my mind of fatal accidents and as I looked for a reason for the delay I never even gave the girl any thought, believing every word when he did finally show and he told me that he had gone to collect her first but his van broke down. When he told me he hadn't known his friend was abroad I believed him and even with the smell of the girl all over him I believed him when he said he hadn't even seen her. I accepted his explanations and as I set the scene that I had earlier enacted in my mind I could not wait to tell him our wonderful news. All I really recall were his words "You stupid little slut" as he slammed the door when he left shouting afterwards "that was it we were finished"

For days after, I was numb and spent most of my time in my room holding my tiny stomach and wondering what now for its contents and how on earth was I going to tell. My parents naturally assumed my misery was due to the recent break-up and tried to comfort me with words like "you'll get over it" and "plenty more fish in the sea" Somehow I cont nued to go about my daily routine whilst managing to conceal the growing bump and the bouts of morning sickness.

Desperate to talk to someone I finally made an appointment to see my doctor. Arrangements were made for me to attend the hospital where I would be having an abortion then apparently all of my problems would be over. Arriving at the hospital I was in pieces when the kind nurse took my hand and told me that I didn't have to go through this and that there were places for single mothers where they could keep their child. My mind was made up my baby was staying with me.

Unable to conceal the growing for much longer, through a friend I managed to tell my mother who said she was surprised and disappointed that I could not tell her myself. She told me it would be okay and that we would sort something out adding that she had no idea what my father would have to say about it.

Sitting like a scolded child in the living room I waited anxiously as she talked to my father in a separate room wondering what the outcome would be. He might as well have had a shotgun as we all bundled into his car to go and tell the proud father and his parents that there was a wedding to be arranged. My ex and I sat in awe as the two sets of parents battled it out, his mother kept going into hysterics and was more worried about what people would say than worrying about me or her son, let alone our unborn child.

Several weeks and chats later a church had been booked a dress made, suits ordered and a hall and reception catered for, without either of us the engaged couple having a say in the matter what so ever. Even the best man and bridesmaid, some friends of his parents were unknown to either of us. As the big day arrived caught up I guess in the thrill of it all, I was dressed made up and paraded in front of family, friends and a photographer whilst my future mother in law appeared to be in her element ordering my own mother about and organising all and everyone in her path.

It was only when finally alone with my father that I realised the horror it all. I told him that there was no way that i could go through with the charade, but even he said I had too. He reminded me the people who had come miles to be there. This wedding must go on and so it did. Even as I trembled walking down that isle I knew I made my father proud and as heads turned to look at me I was again caught up in the fairy tail magic of the whole event.

As the big day arrived caught up I guess in the thrill of it all, I was dressed made up and paraded in front of family, friends and a photographer whilst my future mother in law appeared to be in her element ordering my own mother about and organising all and everyone in her path. It was only when finally alone with my father that I realised the horror of it all, I told him that there was no way that I could go through with this but even he said I had too . He reminded me of the cost and the people that had come miles to be there. This wedding must go on and so it did. Even as I trembled walking down that isle I knew I made my father proud and as heads turned to look at me I was again caught up in the fairy tail magic of the whole event.

Settling into our first home, a caravan, it all felt like a game, ike playing house with real live people. I loved that caravan the serenity and peace that I found there when my now husband had gone to work. It was a place that I could go undisturbed. To tidy and provide meals and comfort for my working man and to prepare for the arrival of our new born child. At last it seemed that I had found the happiness which I had desired only to find over time a black cloud was looming in the form of the mother in law. With her constant meddling and interfering I could feel myself going down in my self esteem as she continued to manipulate her son and took over our lives till they no longer remained our own.

Tensions between the three of us grew and I began to feel trapped by my surroundings and felt suffocated by all the attention his mother was so lavishly trying to inflict upon us. I'd had enough and found myself taking my heavily pregnant body back home to my mum and dad only to be marched straight back to my responsibilities.

As time passed and the nearing of my baby's birth arrived, the atmosphere and surroundings once again changed with everyone caught up in the excitement and anticipation, when I finally went into labour. With my family around me in harmony and the love in all of their eyes as my tiny little son arrived, I felt contentment like none I had never yet experienced. I loved the feel of the warmth and affection that came as they gazed into his tiny face, of the love I felt from my husband, his arms cradling me and our small bundle lay between us both.

MOTHERS RUIN

Once again I had found my hearts desire and as my child developed through his first year I found delight in watching the changes that took place. His first smile, his tiny hand reaching for mine and the way his bright little eyes twinkled when ever he saw my face. This was true love. The tiny boy needed me and I needed him. His night cries becoming totally dependent on me and being only quietened by the comfort of my arms and the warm milk that flowed from my breast.

My husband began to get jealous and angry at the attention our son was getting and at the attention he was not. So much so that he would stay out late and find that attention in the arms of other women. That in its self never seemed to bother me, but I hated the way he smelt of beer and the way he would tell me in graphic detail of the sex he had encountered with any of these women. He had become repulsive to me and the armour around me began to grow stronger as I stood up to his cruel words. Refusing even to bat an eye lid as his fist would crash down on me.

Oh but he was clever sending the blows below face level so that the bruises never showed to the public eye. Becoming the loving family man and doting husband in the eyes of friends and family. As I saw it I had no way out so I would continue to accept this way of life, relishing in the personal joy that I got from my time spent with my son. Eventually though the armour had started to crack as his bullying continued and I began to bite back. Screaming at him and hitting back like a crazed lunatic.

Till his interfering mother would turn up at his request, to protect her son from this animal that he had married. Shouting obscenities at me this woman would stand in front of her son protecting him from my blows. Then one time she snatched my tiny boy from his cot taking him and her own son away from me leaving me sobbing on the floor of my caravan and telling me that I would never get my child back. I felt so alone and not knowing what on earth I could do next I ran the mile to the nearest telephone, trying desperately to contact my parents till eventually they came to my rescue. I felt as proud of my mother as she stood up to the evil woman, picking my baby up and handing him back to me.

Gathering a few pieces together I left the caravan and went home to live with my parent's safe in the knowledge that I could no longer be hurt. Relying heavily on my parent's emotional and financial support I repaid them by cleaning their house and cooking their meals, whilst they both worked. As kind as they were and as much as I appreciated their help after time I began to feel smothered by their rules and their way of life and longed for the freedom of my little caravan and a life of my own.

Funnily enough on some days when they were working my husband would sneak over to see his son and me thus redeveloping our relationship and rekindling a small flame between us. When I announced I was going back to him my mother was shocked and I expect a little angry. My father a man of few words just said he hoped I knew what I was doing and something along the lines of having made my bed I would have to lie on it. My mother said she had washed her hands of me. Of course she hadn't as when my husband found us a nice cottage to rent her and the mother in law put their differences behind them as they rallied round to help us.

Life was grand, my husband worked hard, I kept house parents and in-laws only visited on assigned days and my small boy learnt to walk and talk as he happily played in the small garden. It was two years of bliss that just went pear shaped the moment I announced that I was pregnant again, the arguments restarted, the mother in law interfered and the whole relationship crumbled resulting once again in me and my boy going back to live with my parents. No amount of discussion or secret meetings with my husband seemed to make it better. We drifted as our individual parents then took charge of our lives and our futures became divided. Just as in those early days when they took over with wedding plans now they were organising solicitors and divorces.

The year passed quickly as my developing baby grew safely in my womb and my toddler son and I became closer. I would always tell him that this was his new baby, desperate not to push him away and wanting to develop a bond between them before his sibling arrived. The visits from his father became few and far between and the once doting grandmother chose not to make any contact at all. It was sad for the little boy but he had me and my parents who loved him dearly and soon he would have his own little playmate. Just days before my daughter was born I was given a council house, as much as I had appreciated my parents giving me shelter it was good to have a place of our own.

When my little girl arrived she was beautiful and as I took her home to her brother he at first ran to hide behind a chair, then in the weeks and years that followed he developed a bond with her that remains as special to this day.

A FAMILY MAN

It was when my daughter reached her second year that I developed a friendship with a man who lived in the same area. He had children of a similar age and at first we would chat at the school till before long a friendship developed. His own marriage had reached an end and in time we grew closer until our friendship had become love and then he asked me to marry him.

A small selection of friends and relations attended the registrar office service then later we celebrated in our home. Ours was not a passionate love but we were good friends and he was a good parent to my children. His own children would spend weekends with us and in the years that followed we became a family with the addition of two sons of our own. Most of the eight years that we spent together were probably the happiest of my life. Content with my lot I was blissfully settled with my way of life.

However not so it would seem for my husband who sought excitement and extra marital love in the arms of another woman. As always I found myself dwelling on the sins of the past and looking to blame someone for the things that happened to me. I felt worthless and wondered what I had done that was so bad to drive him away. I had thought I was a good wife the meals were on the table, I kept a tidy house, attended to his every need and even things in the bedroom were as they should be, though at times it was more of a formality than an adventure.

Around this time I had become depressed because I had lost a baby four months before it was due to be born. Then discovering, almost six weeks later that I was expecting again. It was touch and go throughout those nine months till my beautiful son was born by emergency caesarean resulting almost in the loss of his or my own life.

I adored my new son, but was it any wonder that I sufferec a double dose of post natal depression. Devoting my time to my children, I neglected my home and my appearance as I drifted deeper into a more miserable state. Surrounding myself with the love for my children became a safety net for me, so I might have been neglecting my husband in the process. He never discussed anything and I longed to be able to communicate with him, but it was getting so that I was afraid to open my mouth.

On the inside I could see that the sturdy walls of my safeness were slowly crumbling away yet I could or would not do anything to restore them. In an instant he could have put it right had he only talked to me or just held me, I wanted him so badly to want me, but he didn't he wanted her and it was I that pushed him to her. When it all came to light I at first chose to ignore it thinking he might get over it, so long as he remained with us as a family then everything would be okay.

In theory that seemed like a good idea but in practice his responsibilities along with his loyalties were diminishing, as he was happily having his cake and eating it. As he chose to spend more time with his woman and less with his family the tensions grew between us and the cracks started to form.

My own dear eldest son became quite troublesome and distant from his stepfather, my daughter spent more time at her friends than at home, and my two youngest aged just six and three years old really didn't seem to understand at all.

We moved house in an endeavor to try and start over, but a little after a week of being there he was back to his love affair, and I had more than I could stand. So deciding to go it alone with just the children when he was out one day I calmly packed all of his belongings in black bags leaving them on the doorstep locked the house and took my children out.

It wasn't necessarily that cut and dried as naturally arguments followed, and despite him having done the cheating, as far as his sisters were concerned my name was mud for having put him out! I hated him for what he had done to our family and I grew quite bitter towards him when he called to see the children yet I cried alone at night in my bed longing for his warm body to be there beside me once again and wondering what I had done that was so wrong to make him want to leave.

As in all or most cases they say the children suffer and in a way I knew they did. A child needs a father but he had left and moved on with his life. His visits becoming less due to the increasing tension that built up between us and in time the contact between him and the children stopped. Trying to be both parents to them was not always an easy task but I did the best that I could do with the resources that I had and if nothing else I gave them love. There are no rules and raising a family isn't always an easy task but I think as the years have progressed, we have on the whole retained a special bond and are all friends as well as family.

The eldest boy was perhaps the hardest to control, that small child that I had wanted so badly was now turning into a young man, and fighting his own demons. Setting the mould that would shape his future and make or break him. A lot of the time I could see myself in him as he had always been such a shy and quiet child, but retaliation had come in the form of his stepfather's departure. Here was a chance for him to seize the day away from that mans teasing and discipline. In later years my son told me that he had always felt left out by his stepfather, who would to him seem to dote more on his natural sons and at times he would feel as though he never really belonged.

Even more so the man would dote on the one daughter as she became the girl he never had. This caused a slight resentment in that young mans head and though it never broke the bond between him and his sister that little bit of green envy would always be there. Looking at things now and thinking back I wonder how I missed that child's pain, I wonder why I wasn't there! Do we do the best we can and just take things day to day at surface value? If it looks good on the outside then why spoil things. It haunts me that I wasn't stronger for my son, as it perhaps now haunts my own mother that she wasn't stronger for me.

STRUGGLING ON

My boy was now fourteen, at that same vulnerable age that I once was when I ran away with the fairground man. For whatever reasons then, I realise that I was looking to be needed, to be loved, wanting someone to make everything okay. Here was my own dear boy getting caught up in a world of drugs and crime. Getting in with the wrong crowd smoking dope, staying out late, skipping school and generally becoming a bad boy.

Here was I fighting my own demons and struggling to pick myself up after a failing marriage. Trying not only to look after myself and my boy, but my other three children who also needed me. I knew I should have taken the boy into my arms and given him the love and understanding that he craved, but instead I shouted at him and drove a small wedge between us. A wedge that would take him towards his own independence, and a little bit away from me.

I hate the word control but all the same it was something you have a little more of when children are younger and you use it to restore some sort of order. Now as my boy developed his own characteristics my control in many ways was leaving me. No longer being able to tell him bed by a certain time and having him willingly doing it. He was developing attitude and badmouthing me. I felt as though I was losing my lovely boy and I was struggling against being there for him or turning my back against him. Getting conflicting advice from family and I suppose well meaning friends around me who would tell me not to let him out, but how can you imprison a developing boy. Or they would tell me to stick him in a home.

I wanted that baby way back then and I wanted him still now, so I turned a blind eye. I put up with the abuse and bad behavior but I never stopped loving him. Sadly though instead of talking and being close like we used to. He got wilder and I got angrier and a rift developed. This continued for the next three years of his life. After a full blown argument he left the security of his mother's arms, and took himself to live in a hovel of a bed sit that became his new home. I had lost my boy that little boy that I wanted and needed so much and I felt as though it was I that had pushed him away.

Throughout those three years I tried so hard to get it right but I seemed to become like two different people with different emotions and different needs. On the outside I would be a good mother and a doting daughter to my parents, taking everything in my stride and carrying on with the same old grind. People were always singing my praises didn't I keep a lovely house, wasn't I a lovely girl, what a dear little family I had. Yet on the inside I felt so lost empty and so dam lonely.

I would fill that void devoting my life and my time to my children. Forsaking friendships & avoiding social occasions believing that any man I met might treat me badly, abuse me in some way or at the very least leave me. I feared the very thing that I wanted so badly, a soul mate, another half, someone to share my life. As I carried on with my life a depression set in which I would comfort with all the cakes and chocolate that I could get my hands on. I became more depressed at how fat and unattractive I was becoming, and I slowly turned myself into a recluse who would only go out to take her children to school.

My children were my life and my lovely daughter became my strength. At just eleven years old when my husband left, she seemed to grow up over night, helping me see to her younger brothers needs. She would get them ready for school and playgroup in the mornings then help with their supper on an evening and getting them bathed and ready for bed at night. Its not that I didn't want to do it myself it's just that at times I really could not be bothered and would sit glued to the television stuffing my fat face as I wallowed in self pity at the deck life had dealt me.

It was her that the older brother turned to when my back had turned on him, and it was her that over time helped to heal the rift between us bringing us all together again as a family. She was then and still is my strength. In a way it was sad that she was made to be so old at such a young age , but it was who she was and what she did that moulded her into the wonderful mother that she is today, to her own dear children. She has over the years become a loving daughter and best friend to me.

My youngest had perhaps relied on me more than any of them, as he was only baby when his father left and his memories of a life shared with him had all diminished. A quiet little boy, deep thinking and soft hearted. He was happy to play with his brothers and sister but also as happy to play or read alone. I suppose out of all of them he had become dependent on his family, and because he was the baby it was easy for us to all fuss over him, and do things for him rather than let him do things for himself. At times even now he is a bit of a worrier and relies on the feedback from all of us to help him form his decisions in times of crisis. He was though a delightful child as he still is today and has always remained close to me since.

It was my middle son who became my salvation an outgoing cheerful child, my funny lovable little monkey. He loved me I know just as his siblings did but he showed it in a much different way. He could be close and loving at times and was very deep, always retaining his independence. A bit like his sister he was born with an adult mind. I say that he became my salvation as it was he that woke me from the depressive trap that I had fallen into. He saved the reclusive me and brought me back to life.

He did this because he had a best friend whose father had recently left and he pushed me into a friendship with that friend's mother. Like two soul mates we immediately bonded and my life finally started to take off again. Joining Gingerbread a group that specialised in forming contact between lone parent families we mixed with people in the same boat, enjoying get together's and holidays on a regular basis and for much of the time we lived a full and satisfactory existence.

My friend was and still is a very confident outgoing lady who took me under her wing and helped me to regain the confidence that I had lost bringing me back to life and making me proud of who I am and I love her for that. Even though now our lives have changed as lives do. Our sons have grown up and gone their separate ways and our bond has lessened but I love her still. As the saying goes some people drift in and out of our lives throughout its term and they come and go for a reason, some just for a moment and some forever. For whatever reason she came along at just the right time and I am glad she is still around today. When we first met we were acquaintances that knew each other via our sons and when those sons threw us together through shared experiences we became friends.

THE LOVER

During one of our nights out we met up with two brothers that we had known from way back and something clicked between us all. A love affair started between her and one of the brothers and me with the other. I admired her ability to maintain independence and make the most of the passion that she shared with the older brother, and whilst I tried to keep my relationship with the younger brother the same try as I might I could not keep him at arms length. The more I got of him the more that I wanted.

He was the love of my life and will always remain special in my heart and mind. That first night our meeting was casual with general chit chat about how we had been and what we had done with our lives. Throughout the course of the evening he was mingling amongst people and kept coming back to me to hold my hand or chat some more. When he took me for that last slow dance I melted in his arms.

The music played, and the drink numbed my senses but the familiarity that I felt with him was comfortable and I enjoyed his company. All too soon the evening had come to an end. Leaving to get my coat I discovered my friend had gone off for the night with the elder brother, leaving me standing alone bewildered at what to do next. Till the younger brother said I could share his taxi and I left with him, I asked him where he wanted to go and he said "wherever you want to take me" So I took him home.

At first kissing me softly on my neck his mouth along with his hands started to move all over my body , I tingled as I responded and we fell into a frenzy of the gentlest love making that I had ever experienced. Caught in the thrill of it all I felt giddy and light headed till a crowd of butterflies that were spinning in my stomach flew down to my groin, and fluttered in a kind of hysteria that felt almost as though they were escaping from my bottom.

Gradually we fell into sleep and I awoke at dawns light gazing into his sleeping face. Watching his every breath I wished that he would never wake and leave me, as I felt sure that I would never see him again. When he did wake he kissed me softly and we made love again and again and again. He had the bluest eyes and the blackest hair and said whispered the tenderest things. Had I not got to leave for work then I quite happily could have laid with him for the remainder of the day.

He followed me to work, a voluntary job at a charity jumble sale for our lone parents group. Where throughout the course of the event he sat motionless on a chair watching my every move. I tried to get on with the tasks on my agenda but catching glimpses of him in the corner of my eye my responsibilities and concentration right out of the window. I felt silly and excited like a teenage girl and I wanted to be with him alone somewhere and naked. Eventually we shared the remainder of that day with a picnic on a nearby riverbank where we walked and talked and shared more intimate moments. I loved him so much.

Two days passed without a word and my heart sank. I knew that I had come on too strong and frightened him away, I must have seemed desperate. My friend kept her head separate from her heart, why could I not be more like her. I hated myself all those negative thoughts crawled back into my mind and I felt worthless. Three days later he rang me and the cloud that was beginning to smother me lifted as he said that he needed to see me and could we meet later that day.

The hours could not pass quickly enough as I showered and tried a variety of clothes on so that I would be perfect for when we met. At the arranged location I was filled with awe at how the meeting would go what would I say how I should be with him? Then the moment I saw him , his eyes making contact, his friendly smile and his deep husky voice calling my name my insides melted and those tingles came back all over me. Here he was my Butterfly man and as he threw his arms around me he whispered into my ear that he loved me.

In the days and the weeks that followed my love for him grew and I lived for every moment I would see him. He was so gentle and so romantic, sending flowers to my place of work, turning up unexpectedly and whisking me off for the day to go for a meal, to the theater a hotel room or just a walk in the park. If I didn't see him he would always phone just to say hello or he would leave notes of love and special sentiments that I would find on my car after work or my pillow when I went to bed at night so that I would know he was around even when he couldn't see me. This was the stuff that fairy tales were made of how it could be happening to me and what if it ended.

I wished that the bubble would never burst. He would tell me how much he loved me and that we would be together always. He said that he wanted me for his wife and one day we would be together in every sense of the word. When I asked when he would just say "when the time is right" I hung on to his every word and never for a moment doubted him.

There were times when I didn't see him for weeks although he would phone on occasion. Sometimes a postcard or missing you card would drop through the letterbox. When I asked why he stayed away he just said that he had to work. He often went abroad and on a few occasions he had taken me to Germany and Spain with him whilst he wheeled and dealed and did whatever it was that he did.

I never questioned his work, he treat me well when we were together and always had a pocket full of cash. He never hid me to his colleagues in fact quite the opposite always keeping me in the limelight and telling everyone that here I was the love of his life. He was so confident and in turn my own confidence grew I felt good in his presence and I liked the person that I was becoming. My family liked him and although he wasn't with us twenty-four/seven it felt as though he belonged.

For almost two years our lives went on like this with his comings and goings and I took it for what it was as it became a habit. He was never violent or unkind to me in any way and I would say that I had no problem whatsoever with him. Apart that is, from when he would start drinking, he wouldn't stop and after awhile I came to realise that he was alcoholic. For the most part of the relationship I wasn't affected by his drinking sprees as I rarely went for a drink with him.

If I did I certainly wouldn't stay as I would get irritated at how stupid he became, and frustrated because the more I wanted him to leave and come home with me the less cooperative he became. The agitation would grow and I could feel myself getting tense and bitter with him and before long I would snap at him and I would say something nasty, going home alone regretting every word. Then just as I thought it was probably all over and that I would never see him again he would show up with flowers or chocolates. Rekindling the passion that I felt for him within my heart and mind it was as though we had never been apart. As though we had some kind of control over each other we both thrived on the attention we got from our continuous game of cat and mouse.

Life went on and other than the drinking I didn't see any reason why we couldn't be together more permanently and I longed for security by means of marriage. Still he would continue to say that the time wasn't right, and if I probed deeper he would get irritated and walk away from me. Once again I wouldn't see him for days and I would grow frantic with worry wondering where he had gone or if he would even come back. Then when he did we would get back to normal and I was so happy just to have him there but he never said where he had been or discussed the previous arguments.

One such time after our third year together he left in a rush, and I decided to go and find him as I didn't want him missing for days. I scoured his usual haunts till I found him but once again I just wanted him home with me, and he wasn't budging so the tensions grew between us. I stormed out to go home he snatched my car keys and followed me he insisting on driving home to sort this out.

We had barely got two miles up the road when he took a sharp bend and lost control of the car. All I recall is a spinning sensation as the car seemed to flip in mid air and the sound of glass breaking. When it was still again. It felt as though I was in a dream, I was upside down and there was glass and blood everywhere and lights, bright lights, shining into my face. Gathering my senses I saw that the lights were torches, I could see faces and people asking me if I was alright and what was my name. "Oh my God" I shouted "where's my boyfriend.

When I eventually managed to climb out through a side window I saw him lying on the roadside his face covered in blood and he was so still that I felt sure he was dead. I kept kissing his face and telling him to wake up but he wasn't moving and the bloody ambulance men kept telling me to get away. He was unconscious for so long and I just wanted to stay with him whist they cleaned him up and stitched the cuts on his face. I wanted to be there when he woke up.

I ached all over my ribs and my stomach hurt and I felt sick and dizzy. I tried desperately to stay awake but I couldn't and felt myself being whisked away into an adjacent cubicle whilst the medical staff checked me over. Apart from a few bruised ribs and a small cut on my hand I was fine and once they saw that I was alert. I called my eldest son to take me home.

DOWNWARD SPIRAL

On phoning the hospital the following morning I learnt that my partner was stable and awake but remaining on bed rest, so I decided later that day to go and visit him. I wanted so badly to see him and tell him how much that I loved him and was filled with anticipation at the forthcoming visit, as I walked through the door and towards his bed all I could see was the look of horror on his face as he spotted me. It slowly dawned on me that the woman sitting on his bed tightly holding his hand and the two young boys by her side were his wife and his sons. I quickly turned and fled as the tears rolled down my cheeks and a feeling of dread came over me. How could I have been so stupid why would I not know! I felt betrayed and sorry for myself not once giving the wife a thought as it was her that he had really betrayed.

Picking myself up yet again over the weeks to follow I began again to get on with my life. Yet I was grieving inside for him and the love that I had lost, crying alone at night and going from the day to day with the courage and strength that always seemed to come through. My family, my children as always supportive and keeping their opinions about him to themselves lest I should snap at them in an endeavor to blame someone for the hurt that I was going through.

Then just as I was getting there and moving on so to speak, a bouquet of the loveliest red roses arrived and a note that said "I need you" that was it at the drop of a hat I fled back to his arms and the whole thing started over again.

I hated myself for falling into his trap though I never doubted his love for me was true. We just clicked together like pieces in a puzzle, like a coin we were one, but we were both opposite sides

Our time together lasted a further four years but always remaining on a timeshare with his wife and family. Naturally she hated me and who could fault her, but I never felt I was to blame. I told myself he needed me or why would he be with me, I knew that he loved her but I convinced myself it was a different kind of love, and somehow the three of us existed in a lifestyle that suited us all. Till one day I was given a choice he would leave his family and I could join him for the rest of my life.

I wanted so desperately to have a future with him but I knew in my heart that it would never be. Even if he left his family I could never leave mine and even if, as he asked I took them with us I knew that t wouldn't work. For years I had put up with this lifestyle and longed for him to be mine and mine alone, yet when it came to it I couldn't leave my life for him ,and I couldn't ask him to leave his for me, so it was kinder then to let him go. My heart wrenched as I told him it was over and asked him to keep away.

I cried for weeks and my family were angry at him for leaving me they couldn't understand that it was I that told him to go. On the occasions when he did get in touch I would ignore him or try too and in time I found the strength to be without him. Though I never totally escaped as every blue moon when he would get in touch I would go to him and we would spend a day or a night declaring our undying love. Finding some comfort from those times.

He never left the wife and though I never envied her life I was sad for her. I could understand why she stayed I pitied her for she had missed out on so much had she have moved on. It was never a case of competing against her the hardest thing was his love for the drink and if anything it was what kept them together and us apart.

Since then I have found no one to take his place but have had a few tries along the way. A sloppy type that would lavish me with love and attention and at the drop of a hat give me what ever my heart desired , but it didn't desire him and I would feel sick at the thought of spending time with him so I pushed him away.

A homely type, who I was led to believe was proper husband material. Once his feet were firmly under my table and I became more of a mother to him, picking up after him and running around in silly little circles. Till I nagged and nagged till finally I managed to drive him away.

A strong affectionate type that provided me with support and made me feel needed , but in time who became a control freak so that I dare not breath for myself and I lived the life till I could take no more and had to escape when he had almost driven me to the point of killing him.

FINAL WORD

I have always associated men with buses. Strange comparison I know, but think about it, we all want to go somewhere with someone and like those buses they can offer you the scenic route, the rocky road, the road to nowhere, the quick trip, the mystery tour or if we are lucky the journey of a lifetime. I myself have had a few trips, the ones that start off pleasant and comfortable but generally end up a bit of a mystery certainly rocky and on the long or short road to nowhere. Still looking for that journey of a lifetime and until I find it I guess I am going to be getting a lot of rides along the way.

By Audrey Winter

5625928R00026

Printed in Great Britain
by Amazon.co.uk, Ltd.,
Marston Gate.